FREE LOOPS

After working in Back or Front Loops Only on a row or round, there will be a ridge of unused loops. These are called the free loops. Later, when instructed to work in the free loops of the same row or round, work in these loops *(Fig. 1a)*.

When instructed to work in free loops of a chain, work in loop indicated by arrow *(Fig. 1b)*.

Fig. 1a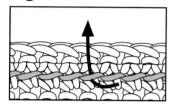

Fig. 1b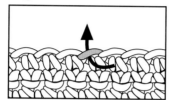

BACK OR FRONT LOOP ONLY

Work only in loop(s) indicated by arrow *(Fig. 2)*.

Fig. 2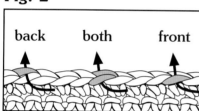

WHIPS

Place two M
Beginning i
both pieces
seam, leaving an ample yarn end to weave in later. Insert the needle from **front** to **back** through **inside** loops on **both** pieces *(Fig. 3)* and pull yarn through. ★ Insert the needle from **front** to **back** through next stitch and pull yarn through; repeat from ★ across to first ch of next ch-2, keeping the sewing yarn fairly loose.

Fig. 3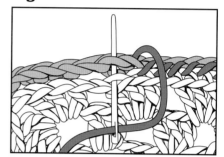

CHAIN STITCH

Chain stitch is worked from right to left. Make all stitches equal in length. Come up at 1 and make a counterclockwise loop with the yarn. Go down at 1 and come up at 2, keeping the yarn below the point of the needle *(Fig. 4a)*. Make a loop with the yarn and go down at 2; come up at 3, keeping yarn below the point of the needle *(Fig. 4b)*. Secure last loop by bringing yarn over loop and down.

Fig. 4a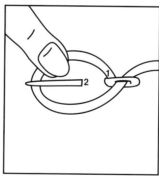

Fig. 4b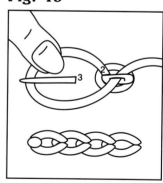

We have made every effort to ensure that these instructions are accurate and complete. We cannot, however, be responsible for human error, typographical mistakes, or variations in individual work.

Production Team: Instructional Editor - Sarah J. Green; Technical Editor - Linda Luder; Artist - Faith Lloyd; and Senior Artist - Diana Sanders.

Instructions tested and photo models made by Raymelle Greening and Dale Potter.

1. PINK POSIES
Shown on page 13.

MATERIALS

Item	Ounces	Yards	Grams	Meters
Top				
Sport Weight Yarn	2¾{3}	250{275}	80{90}	228.5{251.5}
Pants				
Sport Weight Yarn	2½{3}	230{275}	70{90}	210.5{251.5}
Cap				
Sport Weight Yarn	1{1½}	90{135}	30{40}	82.5{123.5}
Booties				
Sport Weight Yarn	¾	70	20	64
Afghan				
Sport Weight Yarn	12	1,090	340	996.5

Crochet hook, size G (4 mm) **or** size needed for gauge
Yarn needle
Sewing needle and thread

½" (12 mm) Buttons - 2
¼" (7 mm) wide Elastic - ½ yard (45.5 cm)
¼" (7 mm) wide Ribbon - 1½ yard (1.5 meters)
Ribbon roses - 12

Finished Size: 3 months and 6 months

Size Note: Instructions are written for size 3 months with size 6 months in braces { }. Instructions will be easier to read if you circle all the numbers pertaining to your size. If only one number is given, it applies to both sizes.

GAUGE: 20 dc and 11 rows = 5" (12.75 cm)

Gauge Swatch: 5" (12.75 cm) square
Ch 22.
Row 1: Dc in fourth ch from hook **(3 skipped chs count as first dc)** and in each ch across: 20 dc.
Rows 2-11: Ch 3 **(counts as first dc)**, turn; dc in next dc and in each dc across.
Finish off.

STITCH GUIDE

CLUSTER (uses one ch-1 sp)
★ YO, insert hook in ch-1 sp indicated, YO and pull up a loop, YO and draw through 2 loops on hook; repeat from ★ 2 times **more**, YO and draw through all 4 loops on hook.

BEGINNING SC DECREASE
Pull up a loop in first 2 sc, YO and draw through all 3 loops on hook **(counts as one sc)**.

SC DECREASE
Pull up a loop in next 2 sc, YO and draw through all 3 loops on hook **(counts as one sc)**.

DC DECREASE (uses next 2 dc)
★ YO, insert hook in **next** dc, YO and pull up a loop, YO and draw through 2 loops on hook; repeat from ★ once **more**, YO and draw through all 3 loops on hook **(counts as one dc)**.

TOP
FRONT
Ch 39{43}.

Row 1: Dc in fourth ch from hook **(3 skipped chs count as first dc, now and throughout)** and in next 11{13} chs, ch 2, skip next 2 chs, sc in next ch, ch 1, skip next 2 chs, (dc, ch 1) 3 times in next ch, skip next 2 chs, sc in next ch, ch 2, skip next 2 chs, dc in last 13{15} chs: 31{35} sts and 6 sps.

Row 2 (Right side)**:** Ch 3 **(counts as first dc, now and throughout)**, turn; dc in next 12{14} dc, skip next ch-2 sp, work Cluster in next ch-1 sp, (ch 3, work Cluster in next ch-1 sp) 3 times, skip next ch-2 sp, dc in last 13{15} dc: 30{34} sts and 3 ch-3 sps.

Note: Loop a short piece of yarn around any stitch to mark Row 2 as **right** side.

Row 3: Ch 3, turn; dc in next 12{14} dc, ch 2, sc in next ch-3 sp, (ch 3, sc in next ch-3 sp) twice, ch 2, skip next Cluster, dc in last 13{15} dc: 29{33} sts and 4 sps.

Row 4: Ch 3, turn; dc in next 12{14} dc, ch 5, skip next ch-2 sp, sc in next ch-3 sp, ch 3, sc in next ch-3 sp, ch 5, skip next ch-2 sp, dc in last 13{15} dc: 28{32} sts and 3 sps.

Row 5: Ch 3, turn; dc in next 12{14} dc, ch 2, sc in next ch-5 sp, ch 1, (dc, ch 1) 3 times in next ch-3 sp, sc in next ch-5 sp, ch 2, dc in last 13{15} dc: 31{35} sts and 6 sps.

Row 6: Ch 3, turn; dc in next 12{14} dc, skip next ch-2 sp, work Cluster in next ch-1 sp, (ch 3, work Cluster in next ch-1 sp) 3 times, skip next ch-2 sp, dc in last 13{15} dc: 30{34} sts and 3 ch-3 sps.

Rows 7-16: Repeat Rows 3-6 twice, then repeat Rows 3 and 4 once **more**: 28{32} sts and 3 sps.

Row 17: Ch 3, turn; dc in next 12{14} dc, place marker in last dc made for st placement, ch 2, sc in next ch-5 sp, ch 1, (dc, ch 1) 3 times in next ch-3 sp, sc in next ch-5 sp, ch 2, dc in last 13{15} dc; do **not** finish off: 31{35} sts and 6 sps.

LEFT NECK SHAPING
Row 1: Ch 3, turn; dc in next 9{11} dc, dc decrease, dc in next dc, leave remaining sts unworked: 12{14} dc.

Row 2: Ch 3, turn; dc decrease, dc in last 9{11} dc: 11{13} dc.

Row 3: Ch 3, turn; dc in next 7{9} dc, dc decrease, dc in last dc; finish off leaving a long end for sewing: 10{12} dc.

RIGHT NECK SHAPING
Row 1: With **right** side facing, join yarn with slip st in marked dc; ch 3, dc decrease, dc in last 10{12} dc: 12{14} dc.

Row 2: Ch 3, turn; dc in next 8{10} dc, dc decrease, dc in last dc: 11{13} dc.

Row 3: Ch 3, turn; dc decrease, dc in last 8{10} dc; finish off leaving a long end for sewing: 10{12} dc.

BACK
Ch 39{43}.

Row 1: Dc in fourth ch from hook and in each ch across: 37{41} dc.

Row 2 (Right side)**:** Ch 3, turn; dc in next dc and in each dc across.

Note: Mark Row 2 as **right** side.

Rows 3-15: Ch 3, turn; dc in next dc and in each dc across; do **not** finish off.

RIGHT NECK
Row 1: Ch 3, turn; dc in next 16{18} dc, leave remaining 20{22} dc unworked: 17{19} dc.

Rows 2-4: Ch 3, turn; dc in next dc and in each dc across.

Row 5: Ch 3, turn; dc in next 9{11} dc; finish off leaving remaining 7 dc unworked: 10{12} dc.

LEFT NECK
Row 1: With **right** side facing, skip first 3 unworked dc on Row 15 and join yarn with slip st in next dc; ch 3, dc in last 16{18} dc: 17{19} dc.

Rows 2-4: Ch 3, turn; dc in next dc and in each dc across.

Finish off.

Row 5: With **right** side facing, skip first 7 dc on Row 4 and join yarn with slip st in next dc; ch 3, dc in last 9{11} dc; finish off: 10{12} dc.

Continued on page 5.

SLEEVE (Make 2)
Ch 27{29}.

Row 1: Dc in fourth ch from hook and in next 5{6} chs, ch 2, skip next 2 chs, sc in next ch, ch 1, skip next 2 chs, (dc, ch 1) 3 times in next ch, skip next 2 chs, sc in next ch, ch 2, skip next 2 chs, dc in last 7{8} chs: 19{21} sts and 6 sps.

Row 2 (Right side)**:** Ch 3, turn; 2 dc in next dc, dc in next 5{6} dc, skip next ch-2 sp, work Cluster in next ch-1 sp, (ch 3, work Cluster in next ch-1 sp) 3 times, skip next ch-2 sp, dc in next 5{6} dc, 2 dc in next dc, dc in last dc: 20{22} sts and 3 ch-3 sps.

Note: Mark Row 2 as **right** side.

Row 3: Ch 3, turn; dc in next 7{8} dc, ch 2, sc in next ch-3 sp, (ch 3, sc in next ch-3 sp) twice, ch 2, skip next Cluster, dc in last 8{9} dc: 19{21} sts and 4 sps.

Row 4: Ch 3, turn; 2 dc in next dc, dc in next 6{7} dc, ch 5, skip next ch-2 sp, sc in next ch-3 sp, ch 3, sc in next ch-3 sp, ch 5, skip next ch-2 sp, dc in next 6{7} dc, 2 dc in next dc, dc in last dc: 20{22} sts and 3 sps.

Row 5: Ch 3, turn; dc in next 8{9} dc, ch 2, sc in next ch-5 sp, ch 1, (dc, ch 1) 3 times in next ch-3 sp, sc in next ch-5 sp, ch 2, dc in last 9{10} dc: 23{25} sts and 6 sps.

Row 6: Ch 3, turn, 2 dc in next dc, dc in next 7{8} dc, skip next ch-2 sp, work Cluster in next ch-1 sp, (ch 3, work Cluster in next ch-1 sp) 3 times, skip next ch-2 sp, dc in next 7{8} dc, 2 dc in next dc, dc in last dc: 24{26} sts and 3 ch-3 sps.

Row 7: Ch 3, turn; dc in next 9{10} dc, ch 2, sc in next ch-3 sp, (ch 3, sc in next ch-3 sp) twice, ch 2, skip next Cluster, dc in last 10{11} dc: 23{25} sts and 4 sps.

Row 8: Ch 3, turn; 2 dc in next dc, dc in next 8{9} dc, ch 5, skip next ch-2 sp, sc in next ch-3 sp, ch 3, sc in next ch-3 sp, ch 5, skip next ch-2 sp, dc in next 8{9} dc, 2 dc in next dc, dc in last dc: 24{26} sts and 3 sps.

Row 9: Ch 3, turn; dc in next 10{11} dc, ch 2, sc in next ch-5 sp, ch 1, (dc, ch 1) 3 times in next ch-3 sp, sc in next ch-5 sp, ch 2, dc in last 11{12} dc: 27{29} sts and 6 sps.

Row 10: Ch 3, turn; dc in next 10{11} dc, skip next ch-2 sp, work Cluster in next ch-1 sp, (ch 3, work Cluster in next ch-1 sp) 3 times, skip next ch-2 sp, dc in last 11{12} dc: 26{28} sts and 3 ch-3 sps.

Row 11: Ch 3, turn; dc in next 10{11} dc, ch 2, sc in next ch-3 sp, (ch 3, sc in next ch-3 sp) twice, ch 2, skip next Cluster, dc in last 11{12} dc; finish off leaving a long end for sewing: 25{27} sts and 4 sps.

FINISHING
Sew shoulder seams.

Sew Sleeves to Top, matching center sc on Sleeve to shoulder seam and beginning 4{4 1/4}"/10{11} cm down from seam.

Sew underarm and side in one continuous seam.

PLACKET
Right Side

Row 1: With **right** side facing and working in end of rows along Right Neck edge, join yarn with sc in top of first dc on Row 4 *(see Joining With Sc, page 1)*, work 8 sc evenly spaced across: 9 sc.

Row 2 (Buttonhole row)**:** Ch 1, turn; sc in first 2 sc, ch 2, skip next sc (buttonhole), sc in next 4 sc, ch 2, skip next sc (buttonhole), sc in last sc: 7 sc and 2 ch-2 sps.

Row 3: Ch 1, turn; sc in each sc and in each ch-2 sp across; finish off.

Left Side

Row 1: With **right** side facing and working in end of rows along Left Neck edge, join yarn with sc in Row 1; work 8 sc evenly spaced across: 9 sc.

Rows 2 and 3: Ch 1, turn; sc in each sc across; at end of Row 3, do **not** finish off.

NECK TRIM
Ch 1, do **not** turn; sc in side of last sc on Row 3 of Left Side, ch 3, skip next row, sc in end of next row, ch 3, skip next dc, (sc in next dc, ch 3, skip next dc) 3 times, sc in end of Row 5 on Left Neck edge, ch 3, skip seam, (sc in end of next row, ch 3) 3 times; working in sps across Row 17 of Front, (sc in next sp, ch 3) 6 times; (sc in end of next row, ch 3) 3 times, skip seam, sc in end of next row, ch 3, skip first unworked dc on Row 4 of Right Neck edge, (sc in next dc, ch 3, skip next dc) 3 times, sc in end of next row, skip next row, sc in end of last row; finish off.

BOTTOM TRIM

Rnd 1: With **right** side facing, join yarn with sc in right seam, ch 3; working in free loops of beginning ch *(Fig. 1b, page 2)*, skip ch at base of first dc, (sc in next ch, ch 3, skip next ch) 6{7} times, (sc in next sp, ch 3) 4 times, skip ch at base of next dc, (sc in next ch, ch 3, skip next ch) 6{7} times, sc in left seam, ch 3, skip ch at base of next dc, sc in next ch, (ch 3, skip next ch, sc in next ch) across to last ch, ch 1, skip last ch, hdc in first sc to form last ch-3 sp.

Rnds 2-5: Ch 1, sc in last ch-3 sp made, (ch 3, sc in next ch-3 sp) around, ch 1, hdc in first sc to form last ch-3 sp.

Rnd 6: Ch 1, sc in last ch-3 sp made, ch 3, (sc in next ch-3 sp, ch 3) around; join with slip st to first sc, finish off.

SLEEVE TRIM

Size 3 Months Only

With **right** side facing, join yarn with sc in seam, ch 3; working in free loops of beginning ch, skip ch at base of first dc, (sc in next ch, ch 3, skip next ch) 3 times, (sc in next sp, ch 3) 4 times, skip ch at base of next dc, (sc in next ch, ch 3, skip next ch) 3 times; join with slip st to first sc, finish off.

Repeat on second Sleeve.

Size 6 Months Only

Rnd 1: With **right** side facing, join yarn with sc in seam, ch 3; working in free loops of beginning ch, skip ch at base of first dc, sc in next ch, ch 3, (skip next ch, sc in next ch, ch 3) 3 times, (sc in next sp, ch 3) 4 times, sc in ch at base of next dc, (ch 3, skip next ch, sc in next ch) 3 times, ch 1, skip last ch, hdc in first sc to form last ch-3 sp.

Rnd 2: Ch 1, sc in last ch-3 sp made, (ch 3, sc in next ch-3 sp) around, ch 1, hdc in first sc to form last ch-3 sp.

Rnd 3: Ch 1, sc in last ch-3 sp made, ch 3, (sc in next ch-3 sp, ch 3) around; join with slip st to first sc, finish off.

Repeat on second Sleeve.

Lapping right side over left, sew bottom edges of Placket to skipped dc on Row 15 of Back.

Sew buttons to Placket opposite buttonholes.

Using photo as a guide for placement, sew three ribbon roses to Front and one to each Sleeve.

PANTS

BODY

Ch 74{82}; being careful not to twist ch, join with slip st to form a ring.

Rnd 1 (Right side)**:** Ch 3 **(counts as first dc, now and throughout)**, dc in next ch and in each ch around; join with slip st to first dc: 74{82} dc.

Note: Loop a short piece of yarn around first dc to mark Rnd 1 as **right** side and back of piece.

Rnds 2 thru 14{16}: Ch 3, dc in next dc and in each dc around; join with slip st to first dc, do **not** finish off.

RIGHT LEG

Rnd 1: Skip next 37{41} dc, slip st in next dc, ch 3, dc in next 36{40} dc; join with slip st to first dc: 37{41} dc.

Rnd 2 (Decrease row)**:** Ch 3, dc decrease, dc in next dc and in each dc around to last 3 dc, dc decrease, dc in last dc; join with slip st to first dc: 35{39} dc.

Rnds 3 and 4: Ch 3, dc in next dc and in each dc around; join with slip st to first dc.

Rnd 5 (Decrease row)**:** Ch 3, dc decrease, dc in next dc and in each dc around to last 3 dc, dc decrease, dc in last dc; join with slip st to first dc: 33{37} dc.

Rnd 6: Ch 3, dc in next dc and in each dc around; join with slip st to first dc.

Rnds 7 thru 14{16}: Repeat Rows 2-6, 1{2} times; then repeat Rows 2-4, 1{0} time(s) **more** *(see Zeros, page 1)*: 27{29} dc.

Trim: Ch 1, pull up a loop in same st as joining and in next dc, YO and draw through all 3 loops on hook, ch 3, skip next dc, ★ sc in next dc, ch 3, skip next dc; repeat from ★ around; join with slip st to first st, finish off.

LEFT LEG

Rnd 1: With **right** side facing, join yarn with slip st in first unworked dc on Row 14{16} of Body; ch 3, dc in next dc and in each dc around; join with slip st to first dc: 37{41} dc.

Complete same as Right Leg.

Continued on page 7.

WAISTBAND

Cut elastic to waist measurement plus 1" (2.5 cm). Overlap edges of elastic 1" (2.5 cm) and sew together.

Rnd 1: With **right** side facing, working in free loops of beginning ch *(Fig. 1b, page 2)* **and** around elastic, join yarn with sc in any ch *(see Joining With Sc, page 1)*; sc in each ch around; join with slip st to first sc: 74{82} sc.

Rnd 2: Ch 1, sc in same st, ch 3, skip next sc, ★ sc in next sc, ch 3, skip next sc; repeat from ★ around; join with slip st to first sc, finish off.

CAP
BODY

Ch 54{58} **loosely**; being careful not to twist ch, join with slip st to form a ring.

Rnd 1 (Right side)**:** Ch 3 **(counts as first dc, now and throughout)**, dc in next ch and in each ch around; join with slip st to first dc: 54{58} dc.

Note: Loop a short piece of yarn around any stitch to mark Rnd 1 as **right** side.

Rnds 2 thru 12{13}: Ch 3, dc in next dc and in each dc around; join with slip st to first dc.

Finish off.

BRIM

Rnd 1: With **wrong** side facing and working in free loops of beginning ch *(Fig. 1b, page 2)*, join yarn with sc in first ch *(see Joining With Sc, page 1)*; ★ ch 3, skip next ch, sc in next ch; repeat from ★ around to last ch, ch 1, skip last ch, hdc in first sc to form last ch-3 sp.

Rnds 2 thru 5{6}: Ch 1, sc in last ch-3 sp made, (ch 3, sc in next ch-3 sp) around, ch 1, hdc in first sc to form last ch-3 sp.

Rnd 6{7}: Ch 1, sc in same sp, ch 3, (sc in next ch-3 sp, ch 3) around; join with slip st to first sc, finish off.

Weave an 18" (45.5 cm) length of ribbon through sts on Rnd 11{12} of Cap Body. Draw ribbon up tightly and tie ends into a bow.

Turn Brim to right side. Using photo as a guide for placement, sew ribbon rose to Brim.

BOOTIES
SOLE

Beginning at toe, ch 7{8}.

Row 1 (Wrong side)**:** Sc in second ch from hook and in each ch across: 6{7} sc.

Note: Loop a short piece of yarn around **back** of any stitch to mark **right** side.

Rows 2 thru 14{16}: Ch 1, turn; sc in each sc across.

Row 15{17}: Ch 1, turn; work beginning sc decrease, sc in next 2{3} sc, sc decrease: 4{5} sc.

Row 16{18}: Ch 1, turn; work beginning sc decrease, sc in next 0{1} sc *(see Zeros, page 1)*, sc decrease: 2{3} sc.

Edging: Ch 1, do **not** turn; work 19{20} sc evenly spaced across end of rows; sc in free loop of each ch across beginning ch *(Fig. 1b, page 2)*; work 19{20} sc evenly spaced across end of rows; sc in last 2{3} sc; join with slip st to first sc, finish off: 46{50} sc.

Place marker in 10th{11th} sc before joining.

INSTEP

Ch 7{8}.

Row 1: Sc in second ch from hook and in each ch across: 6{7} sc.

Row 2: Ch 1, turn; 2 sc in first sc, sc in each sc across to last sc, 2 sc in last sc: 8{9} sc.

Rows 3 thru 9{10}: Ch 1, turn; sc in each sc across; at end of Row 9{10}, do **not** finish off.

SIDES

Ch 11{12}, place marker in last ch made for Cuff placement, ch 11, turn; being careful not to twist ch, join with slip st to last sc on Row 9{10}: 22{23} chs.

Rnd 1 (Right side)**:** Ch 1, sc in end of each row across Instep; sc in free loop of each ch across beginning ch; sc in end of each row across Instep, sc in each ch around; join with slip st to first sc: 46{50} sc.

Note: Mark Rnd 1 as **right** side.

Rnds 2-4: Ch 1, sc in same st and in each sc around; join with slip st to first sc.

Rnd 5 (Joining rnd)**:** Ch 1, **turn**; with **right** side of Sole facing and holding **wrong** sides of Sole and Instep together, matching marked sc on Sole to first sc on Sides and working through **both** thicknesses, sc in same st and in each sc around; join with slip st to first sc, finish off.

CUFF

Rnd 1: With **right** side facing and working in free loops of ch on Sides, join yarn with sc in marked ch *(see Joining With Sc, page 1)*; sc in next 10{11} chs; sc in each sc across last row of Instep; sc in each ch around; join with slip st to first sc: 30{32} sc.

Rnd 2 (Eyelet rnd)**:** Ch 4 **(counts as first dc plus ch 1)**, skip next sc, ★ dc in next sc, ch 1, skip next sc; repeat from ★ around; join with slip st to first dc: 15{16} ch-1 sps.

Rnd 3: Ch 1, sc in same st, (ch 3, sc in next dc) around, ch 1, hdc in first sc to form last ch-3 sp.

Rnd 4: Ch 1, sc in last ch-3 sp made, (ch 3, sc in next ch-3 sp) around, ch 1, hdc in first sc to form last ch-3 sp.

Rnd 5: Ch 1, sc in last ch-3 sp made, ch 3, (sc in next ch-3 sp, ch 3) around; join with slip st to first sc, finish off.

Sew one ribbon rose to each Instep.

Weave an 18" (45.5 cm) length of ribbon through Eyelet rnd and tie ends into a bow.

AFGHAN

Finished Size: 36" x 34" (91.5 cm x 86.5 cm)

BODY

Ch 151, place marker in third ch from hook for st placement.

Row 1: Dc in fourth ch from hook **(3 skipped chs count as first dc)** and in next 3 chs, ★ ch 2, skip next 2 chs, sc in next ch, ch 1, skip next 2 chs, (dc, ch 1) 3 times in next ch, skip next 2 chs, sc in next ch, ch 2, skip next 2 chs, dc in next 5 chs; repeat from ★ across: 95 sts and 54 sps.

Row 2 (Right side)**:** Ch 3 **(counts as first dc, now and throughout)**, turn; dc in next 4 dc, ★ skip next ch-2 sp, work Cluster in next ch-1 sp, (ch 3, work Cluster in next ch-1 sp) 3 times, skip next ch-2 sp, dc in next 5 dc; repeat from ★ across: 86 sts and 27 ch-3 sps.

Note: Loop a short piece of yarn around any stitch to mark Row 2 as **right** side.

Row 3: Ch 3, turn; dc in next 4 dc, ★ ch 2, sc in next ch-3 sp, (ch 3, sc in next ch-3 sp) twice, ch 2, skip next Cluster, dc in next 5 dc; repeat from ★ across: 77 sts and 36 sps.

Row 4: Ch 3, turn; dc in next 4 dc, ★ ch 5, skip next ch-2 sp, sc in next ch-3 sp, ch 3, sc in next ch-3 sp, ch 5, skip next ch-2 sp, dc in next 5 dc; repeat from ★ across: 68 sts and 27 sps.

Row 5: Ch 3, turn; dc in next 4 dc, ★ ch 2, sc in next ch-5 sp, ch 1, (dc, ch 1) 3 times in next ch-3 sp, sc in next ch-5 sp, ch 2, dc in next 5 dc; repeat from ★ across: 95 sts and 54 sps.

Row 6: Ch 3, turn; dc in next 4 dc, ★ skip next ch-2 sp, work Cluster in next ch-1 sp, (ch 3, work Cluster in next ch-1 sp) 3 times, skip next ch-2 sp, dc in next 5 dc; repeat from ★ across: 86 sts and 27 ch-3 sps.

Rows 7-71: Repeat Rows 3-6, 16 times; then repeat Row 3 once **more**; do **not** finish off: 77 sts and 36 sps.

BORDER

Rnd 1: Ch 1, turn; (sc, ch 3) twice in first dc, † (skip next dc, sc in next dc, ch 3) twice, (sc in next sp, ch 3) 4 times, sc in next dc, ch 3 †; repeat from † to † across to last 4 dc, skip next dc, sc in next dc, ch 3, skip next dc, (sc, ch 3) twice in last dc; working in end of rows, sc in same row, ch 3, (sc in next row, ch 3) across; working in free loops of beginning ch *(Fig. 1b, page 2)*, (sc, ch 3) twice in marked ch, ★ (skip next ch, sc in next ch, ch 3) twice, (sc in next sp, ch 3) 4 times, sc in ch at base of next dc, ch 3; repeat from ★ across to last 4 chs, skip next ch, sc in next ch, ch 3, skip next ch, (sc, ch 3) twice in last ch; working in end of rows, sc in same row, ch 3, (sc in next row, ch 3) across; join with slip st to first sc.

Rnds 2-7: Slip st in first corner ch-3 sp, ch 1, (sc, ch 3) twice in same sp, ★ (sc in next ch-3 sp, ch 3) across to next corner ch-3 sp, (sc, ch 3) twice in corner ch-3 sp; repeat from ★ 2 times **more**, (sc in next ch-3 sp, ch 3) across; join with slip st to first sc.

Finish off.

Using photo as a guide for placement, sew a ribbon rose in each corner of Afghan Body.

2. SWEETHEART ROSES

Shown on Front Cover.

MATERIALS

Item	Ounces	Yards	Grams	Meters
Jacket				
Green Sport Weight Yarn	3½{4}	320{365}	100{110}	292.5{334}
Pink Fingering Weight Yarn	¼	45	5	41
Bubble Suit				
Green Sport Weight Yarn	6½{7½}	590{685}	180{210}	539.5{626.5}
Pink Fingering Weight Yarn	¼	45	5	41
Booties				
Green Sport Weight Yarn	¾{1}	70{90}	20{30}	64{82.5}
Pink Fingering Weight Yarn		30{35}		27.5{32}
Headband				
Green Fingering Weight Yarn		15		13.5
Pink Fingering Weight Yarn		15		13.5
Afghan				
Green Sport Weight Yarn	12	1,090	340	996.5
Pink Sport Weight Yarn	4	365	110	334
Pink Fingering Weight Yarn	½	85	15	77.5

Crochet hooks, sizes D (3.25 mm) **and** G (4 mm)
  or sizes needed for gauge
Yarn needle
Sewing needle and thread

½" (12 mm) Buttons - 8
½" (12 mm) wide Ribbon - 12" (30.5 cm)
¼" (7 mm) wide Ribbon - 4 yards (3.5 meters)

Finished Size: 3 months and 6 months

Size Note: Instructions are written for size 3 months with size 6 months in braces { }. Instructions will be easier to read if you circle all the numbers pertaining to your size. If only one number is given, it applies to both sizes.

GAUGE: With Sport Weight Yarn and larger size hook, 20 dc and 11 rows = 5" (12.75 cm)

Gauge Swatch: 5" (12.75 cm) square
With Sport Weight Yarn and larger size hook, ch 22.
Row 1: Dc in fourth ch from hook **(3 skipped chs count as first dc)** and in each ch across: 20 dc.
Rows 2-11: Ch 3 **(counts as first dc)**, turn; dc in next dc and in each dc across.
Finish off.

STITCH GUIDE

BEGINNING SC DECREASE
Pull up a loop in first 2 sc, YO and draw through all 3 loops on hook **(counts as one sc)**.

SC DECREASE
Pull up a loop in next 2 sc, YO and draw through all 3 loops on hook **(counts as one sc)**.

BEGINNING POPCORN (uses one st)
Ch 3 **(counts as first dc)**, work 3 dc in st indicated, drop loop from hook, insert hook in first dc of 4-dc group, hook dropped loop and draw through.

POPCORN (uses one sc)
Work 4 dc in sc indicated, drop loop from hook, insert hook in first dc of 4-dc group, hook dropped loop and draw through.

BEGINNING CLUSTER (uses one sp)
Ch 2, ★ YO, insert hook in **same** sp, YO and pull up a loop, YO and draw through 2 loops on hook; repeat from ★ once **more**, YO and draw through all 3 loops on hook.

CLUSTER (uses one sp)
★ YO, insert hook in sp indicated, YO and pull up a loop, YO and draw through 2 loops on hook; repeat from ★ 2 times **more**, YO and draw through all 4 loops on hook.

JACKET

Use Green Sport Weight Yarn and larger size hook throughout Jacket unless otherwise specified.

YOKE
Ch 44.

Row 1 (Right side)**:** Dc in fourth ch from hook **(3 skipped chs count as first dc)** and in next 2 chs, (2 dc, ch 1, 2 dc) in next ch, ★ dc in next 10 chs, (2 dc, ch 1, 2 dc) in next ch; repeat from ★ 2 times **more**, dc in last 4 chs: 54 dc.

Note: Loop a short piece of yarn around any stitch to mark Row 1 as **right** side.

Row 2: Ch 3 **(counts as first dc, now and throughout)**, turn; ★ dc in next dc and in each dc across to next ch-1 sp, (2 dc, ch 1, 2 dc) in ch-1 sp; repeat from ★ 3 times **more**, dc in last 6 dc: 70 dc.

Rows 3-6: Ch 3, turn; ★ dc in next dc and in each dc across to next ch-1 sp, (2 dc, ch 1, 2 dc) in ch-1 sp; repeat from ★ 3 times **more**, dc in next dc and in each dc across: 134 dc.

BODY

Row 1: Ch 3, turn; ★ dc in next dc and in each dc across to next ch-1 sp, 3 dc in ch-1 sp, skip next 34 dc (armhole), 3 dc in next ch-1 sp; repeat from ★ once **more**, dc in last 16 dc: 78 dc.

Rows 2 thru 3{4}: Ch 3, turn; dc in next dc and in each dc across.

Row 4{5}: Ch 1, turn; 2 sc in first dc, sc in next dc and in each dc across: 79 sc.

Row 5{6}: Ch 3, turn; ★ skip next sc, (2 dc, ch 1, 2 dc) in next sc; repeat from ★ across to last 2 sc, skip next sc, dc in last sc: 38 ch-1 sps.

Rows 6{7} and 7{8}: Ch 3, turn; (2 dc, ch 1, 2 dc) in next ch-1 sp and in each ch-1 sp across, dc in last dc.

Finish off.

LEFT SLEEVE

Rnd 1: With **right** side facing, join yarn with slip st in end of Body Row 1 on left front; ch 3, (dc, ch 1, 2 dc) in same sp, working in skipped dc on Row 6 of Yoke, ★ skip next 2 dc, (2 dc, ch 1, 2 dc) in next dc; repeat from ★ across to last dc, skip last dc, (2 dc, ch 1, 2 dc) in end of Body Row 1 on back; join with slip st to first dc: 13 ch-1 sps.

Rnds 2 thru 9{10}: Slip st in next dc and in next ch-1 sp; ch 3, (dc, ch 1, 2 dc) in same sp, (2 dc, ch 1, 2 dc) in next ch-1 sp and in each ch-1 sp around; join with slip st to first dc.

Rnd 10{11}: Slip st in next dc and in next ch-1 sp, ch 1, sc in same sp and in each ch-1 sp around; join with slip st to first sc: 13 sc.

Rnd 11{12}: Ch 3, dc in same st, ★ dc in next 2 sc, 2 dc in next sc; repeat from ★ around; join with slip st to first dc: 18 dc.

Rnd 12{13}: Ch 1, sc in same st and in each dc around; join with slip st to first sc, finish off.

Rnd 13{14}: With **right** side facing and using smaller size hook, join Pink Fingering Weight Yarn with sc in any sc *(see Joining With Sc, page 1)*; ch 3, sc in same st, (sc, ch 3, sc) in next sc and in each sc around; join with slip st to first sc, finish off.

RIGHT SLEEVE

Rnd 1: With **right** side facing, join yarn with slip st in end of Body Row 1 on back; ch 3, (dc, ch 1, 2 dc) in same sp, working in skipped dc on Row 6 of Yoke, ★ skip next 2 dc, (2 dc, ch 1, 2 dc) in next dc; repeat from ★ across to last dc, skip last dc, (2 dc, ch 1, 2 dc) in end of Body Row 1 on right front; join with slip st to first dc: 13 ch-1 sps.

Complete same as Left Sleeve.

Continued on page 11.

FINISHING
BUTTON BAND
Row 1: With **right** side facing and working in end of rows along left front edge, join yarn with sc in Row 1; work 23{26} sc evenly spaced across: 24{27} sc.

Rows 2 and 3: Ch 1, turn; sc in each sc across.

Finish off.

BUTTONHOLE BAND
Row 1: With **right** side facing and working in end of rows along right front edge, join yarn with sc in last row of Body; work 23{26} sc evenly spaced across: 24{27} sc.

Row 2 (Buttonhole row)**:** Ch 1, turn; sc in first sc, ch 2, skip next sc (buttonhole), ★ sc in next 6{7} sc, ch 2, skip next sc (buttonhole); repeat from ★ 2 times **more**, sc in last sc.

Row 3: Ch 1, turn; sc in each sc and in each ch-2 sp across; do **not** finish off.

NECK TRIM
Row 1: Ch 1, do **not** turn; working in end of rows along Buttonhole Band, skip first row, sc in next 2 rows; working in free loops of beginning ch **(Fig. 1b, page 2)**, sc in first 4 chs, skip next ch, ★ sc in next 10 chs, skip next ch; repeat from ★ 2 times **more**, sc in last 4 chs; sc in next 3 rows on Button Band; finish off: 43 sc.

Row 2: With **right** side facing and using smaller size hook, join Pink Fingering Weight Yarn with sc in first sc; ch 3, sc in same st, ★ skip next sc, (sc, ch 3, sc) in next sc; repeat from ★ across; finish off.

ROSE (Make 5)
With Pink Fingering Weight yarn and smaller size hook, ch 4; join with slip st to form a ring.

Rnd 1 (Right side)**:** Ch 1, (sc in ring, ch 3) 5 times; join with slip st to first sc: 5 ch-3 sps.

Note: Mark Rnd 1 as **right** side.

Rnd 2: Ch 1, (sc, 5 dc, sc) in first ch-3 sp and in each ch-3 sp around; join with slip st to first sc: 5 petals.

Rnd 3: Ch 1, working in **front** of petals, sc around first sc on Rnd 1, ch 2, (sc around next sc on Rnd 1, ch 2) around; join with slip st to first sc: 5 ch-2 sps.

Rnd 4: Ch 1, (sc, 3 dc, sc) in first ch-2 sp and in each ch-2 sp around; join with slip st to first sc, finish off leaving a long end for sewing.

Using photo as a guide for placement, sew three Roses to Buttonhole Band and sew one Rose to each Sleeve.

Sew buttons to Button Band opposite buttonholes.

Weave an 18" (45.5 cm) length of $1/4$" (7 mm) wide ribbon through dc on Rnd 11{12} of each Sleeve; tie ends into a bow.

Tie a 12" (30.5 cm) length of $1/2$" (12 mm) wide ribbon into a bow; tack to center back on Row 2 of Body.

BUBBLE SUIT
Use Green Sport Weight Yarn and larger size hook throughout Bubble Suit unless otherwise specified.

FRONT YOKE
Ch 25{27}.

Row 1 (Right side)**:** Sc in second ch from hook and in each ch across: 24{26} sc.

Note: Loop a short piece of yarn around any stitch to mark Row 1 as **right** side.

Rows 2-4: Ch 1, turn; sc in each sc across.

Row 5: Ch 3 **(counts as first dc, now and throughout)**, turn; working in Back Loops Only **(Fig. 2, page 2)**, dc in same st and in each sc across to last sc, 2 dc in last sc: 26{28} dc.

Rows 6-8: Ch 3, turn; working in both loops, dc in same st and in each dc across to last dc, 2 dc in last dc: 32{34} dc.

Row 9: Ch 3, turn; 2 dc in same st, dc in next dc and in each dc across to last dc, 3 dc in last dc: 36{38} dc.

Size 3 Months Only: Finish off.

Size 6 Months Only - Row 10: Ch 3, turn; dc in next dc and in each dc across; finish off.

LEFT SHOULDER
Row 1: With **right** side of Front Yoke facing and working in free loops of beginning ch **(Fig. 1b, page 2)**, join yarn with sc in first ch **(see Joining With Sc, page 1)**; sc in next 5 chs, leave remaining chs unworked: 6 sc.

Rows 2 thru 7{9}: Ch 1, turn; sc in each sc across.

Finish off.

Row 8{10}: Ch 6{7}; with **wrong** side of Left Shoulder facing, sc in each sc across; do **not** finish off: 6 sc and 6{7} chs.

LEFT BACK YOKE

Row 1: Ch 1, turn; sc in each sc and in each ch across: 12{13} sc.

Rows 2-4: Ch 1, turn; sc in each sc across.

Row 5: Ch 3, turn; dc in Back Loop Only of same st and each sc across: 13{14} dc.

Row 6: Ch 3, turn; working in both loops, dc in next dc and in each dc across to last dc, 2 dc in last dc: 14{15} dc.

Row 7: Ch 3, turn; dc in same st and in each dc across: 15{16} dc.

Row 8: Ch 3, turn; dc in next dc and in each dc across to last dc, 2 dc in last dc: 16{17} dc.

Row 9: Ch 3, turn; 2 dc in same st, dc in next dc and in each dc across: 18{19} dc.

Size 3 Months Only: Finish off.

Size 6 Months Only - Row 10: Ch 3, turn; dc in next dc and in each dc across; finish off.

RIGHT SHOULDER

Row 1: With **right** side of Front Yoke facing and working in free loops of beginning ch, skip 12{14} chs from Left Shoulder and join yarn with sc in next ch; sc in next 5 chs: 6 sc.

Rows 2 thru 8{10}: Ch 1, turn; sc in each sc across; do **not** finish off.

RIGHT BACK YOKE

Row 1: Ch 7{8}, turn; sc in second ch from hook and in each ch and each sc across: 12{13} sc.

Rows 2-4: Ch 1, turn; sc in each sc across.

Row 5: Ch 3, turn; working in Back Loops Only, dc in next sc and in each sc across to last sc, 2 dc in last sc: 13{14} dc.

Row 6: Ch 3, turn; dc in both loops of same st and each dc across: 14{15} dc.

Row 7: Ch 3, turn; dc in next dc and in each dc across to last dc, 2 dc in last dc: 15{16} dc.

Row 8: Ch 3, turn; dc in same st and in each dc across: 16{17} dc.

Row 9: Ch 3, turn; 2 dc in same st, dc in next dc and in each dc across: 18{19} dc.

Size 3 Months Only: Finish off.

Size 6 Months Only - Row 10: Ch 3, turn; dc in next dc and in each dc across; finish off.

BODY

Row 1: With **right** side facing, join yarn with slip st in first dc on Right Back Yoke; ch 3, dc in same st and in each dc across; with **right** side of Front Yoke facing, dc in each dc across; with **right** side of Left Back Yoke facing, dc in each dc across to last dc, 2 dc in last dc: 74{78} dc.

Row 2: Ch 3, turn; (dc, ch 1, dc) in next dc, ★ skip next dc, (dc, ch 1, dc) in next dc; repeat from ★ across to last 2 dc, skip next dc, dc in last dc: 36{38} ch-1 sps.

Rows 3 thru 8{10}: Ch 3, turn; (2 dc, ch 1, 2 dc) in next ch-1 sp and in each ch-1 sp across, dc in last dc.

Begin working in rounds.

Rnd 1: Ch 3, turn; (2 dc, ch 1, 2 dc) in next ch-1 sp and in each ch-1 sp across, dc in last dc, ch 3 (placket); join with slip st to first dc: 36{38} ch-1 sps and one ch-3.

Rnd 2: Do **not** turn; slip st in next 2 dc and in next ch-1 sp, ch 3, (dc, ch 1, 2 dc) in same sp, (2 dc, ch 1, 2 dc) in next ch-1 sp and in each ch-1 sp around to ch-3, (2 dc, ch 1, 2 dc) in center ch of ch-3; join with slip st to first dc: 37{39} ch-1 sps.

Rnd 3: Slip st in next dc and in next ch-1 sp, ch 3, (dc, ch 1, 2 dc) in same sp, (2 dc, ch 1, 2 dc) in next ch-1 sp and in each ch-1 sp around to last ch-1 sp, 2 dc in last ch-1 sp, (ch 1, 2 dc in same sp) twice; join with slip st to first dc: 38{40} ch-1 sps.

Rnds 4-8: Slip st in next dc and in next ch-1 sp, ch 3, (dc, ch 1, 2 dc) in same sp, (2 dc, ch 1, 2 dc) in next ch-1 sp and in each ch-1 sp around; join with slip st to first dc, do **not** finish off.

FIRST LEG

Rnd 1: Slip st in next dc and in next ch-1 sp, ch 3, (dc, ch 1, 2 dc) in same sp, (2 dc, ch 1, 2 dc) in next 18{19} ch-1 sps, leave remaining sps unworked; join with slip st to first dc: 19{20} ch-1 sps.

Rnds 2 thru 11{13}: Slip st in next dc and in next ch-1 sp, ch 3, (dc, ch 1, 2 dc) in same sp, (2 dc, ch 1, 2 dc) in each ch-1 sp around; join with slip st to first dc.

Continued on page 15.

Rnd 12{14}: Slip st in next dc and in next ch-1 sp, ch 1, sc in same sp and in each ch-1 sp around; join with slip st to first sc: 19{20} sc.

Rnd 13{15}: Ch 3, dc in same st, ★ dc in next 2 sc, 2 dc in next sc; repeat from ★ 5 times **more**, dc in last 0{1} sc *(see Zeros, page 1)*; join with slip st to first dc: 26{27} dc.

Rnd 14{16}: Ch 1, sc in same st and in each dc around; join with slip st to first sc, finish off.

Rnd 15{17}: With **right** side facing and using smaller size hook, join Pink Fingering Weight Yarn with sc in any sc; ch 3, sc in same st, (sc, ch 3, sc) in next sc and in each sc around; join with slip st to first sc, finish off.

SECOND LEG
Rnd 1: With **right** side facing, join yarn with slip st in first skipped ch-1 sp on Rnd 8 of Body; ch 3, (dc, ch 1, 2 dc) in same sp, (2 dc, ch 1, 2 dc) in next 18{19} ch-1 sps; join with slip st to first dc: 19{20} ch-1 sps.

Complete same as First Leg.

Sew opening closed.

FINISHING
RIGHT PLACKET
Row 1: With **right** side facing and working in end of rows across Right Back Yoke and Body, join yarn with sc in Row 1; work 31{35} sc evenly spaced across: 32{36} sc.

Row 2 (Buttonhole row)**:** Ch 1, turn; sc in first 6{10} sc, ch 2, skip next sc (buttonhole), ★ sc in next 7 sc, ch 2, skip next sc (buttonhole); repeat from ★ 2 times **more**, sc in last sc; finish off.

LEFT PLACKET
Row 1: With **right** side facing and working in end of rows on Body and Left Back Yoke, join yarn with sc in last row of Body; work 31{35} sc evenly spaced across: 32{36} sc.

Row 2: Ch 1, turn; sc in each sc across.

Trim: Ch 1, turn; sc in each sc across; sc in end of next 2 rows of Left Placket; working in free loops of chs on Yokes and in end of rows on Shoulders, sc in each ch and in each row across to Right Placket, sc in next 2 rows of Right Placket, sc in each sc and in each ch-2 sp across; finish off.

Armhole Trim: With **right** side facing, join yarn with sc at underarm; work 39{41} sc evenly spaced around; join with slip st to first sc, finish off.

Repeat on second Armhole.

Yoke Ruffle: With **right** side and neck opening facing you and using smaller size hook, join Pink Fingering Weight Yarn with sc in free loop of first sc on Row 4 of Right Back Yoke *(Fig. 1a, page 2)*; ch 3, sc in same st, † working in free loops, (sc, ch 3, sc) in each st across to last sc, sc in last sc, (ch 3, sc in same st) 3 times †; working in Front Loops Only of sc on Armhole Trim *(Fig. 2, page 2)*, (sc, ch 3, sc) in each sc across to free loops of sc on Row 4 of Front Yoke; sc in free loop of first sc, (ch 3, sc in same st) 3 times, repeat from † to † once; working in Front Loops Only of sc on Armhole Trim, (sc, ch 3, sc) in each sc across to free loops of sc on Row 4 of Left Back Yoke; sc in first sc, (ch 3, sc in same st) 3 times, (sc, ch 3, sc) in each sc across; finish off.

Beginning at ankle, weave an 18" (45.5 cm) length of 1/4" (7 mm) wide ribbon through dc on Rnd 13{15} of each Leg; tie ends into a bow.

Make five Roses, page 11. Using photo as a guide for placement, sew three Roses to Front Yoke and one Rose to ankle of each Leg.

Sew buttons to Button Band opposite buttonholes.

BOOTIES
Use Green Sport Weight Yarn and larger size hook throughout Booties unless otherwise specified.

SOLE
Beginning at toe, ch 7{8}.

Row 1 (Wrong side)**:** Sc in second ch from hook and in each ch across: 6{7} sc.

Note: Loop a short piece of yarn around **back** of any stitch on Row 1 to mark **right** side.

Rows 2 thru 14{16}: Ch 1, turn; sc in each sc across.

Row 15{17}: Ch 1, turn; work beginning sc decrease, sc in next 2{3} sc, sc decrease: 4{5} sc.

Row 16{18}: Ch 1, work beginning sc decrease, sc in next 0{1} sc *(see Zeros, page 1)*, sc decrease: 2{3} sc.

Edging: Ch 1, do **not** turn; work 19{20} sc evenly spaced across end of rows; sc in free loop of each ch across beginning ch **(Fig. 1b, page 2)**; work 19{20} sc evenly spaced across end of rows; sc in last 2{3} sc; join with slip st to first sc, finish off: 46{50} sc.

Place marker in 10th{11th} sc before joining.

INSTEP
Ch 7{8}.

Row 1: Sc in second ch from hook and in each ch across: 6{7} sc.

Row 2: Ch 1, turn; 2 sc in first sc, sc in each sc across to last sc, 2 sc in last sc: 8{9} sc.

Rows 3 thru 9{10}: Ch 1, turn; sc in each sc across; at end of Row 9{10}, do **not** finish off.

SIDES
Ch 11{12}, place marker in last ch made for Cuff placement, ch 11, turn; being careful not to twist ch, join with slip st to last sc on Row 9{10}: 22{23} chs.

Rnd 1 (Right side)**:** Ch 1, sc in end of each row across Instep; sc in free loop of each ch across beginning ch; sc in end of each row across Instep, sc in each ch around; join with slip st to first sc: 46{50} sc.

Note: Mark Rnd 1 as **right** side.

Rnds 2-4: Ch 1, sc in same st and in each sc around; join with slip st to first sc.

Rnd 5 (Joining rnd)**:** Ch 1; holding **wrong** sides of Instep and Sole together, matching first sc on Sides to marked sc on Sole and working through **both** thicknesses, sc in same st and in each sc around; join with slip st to first sc, finish off.

Rnd 6: With **right** side facing and smaller size hook, join Pink Fingering Weight Yarn with sc in any sc *(see Joining With Sc, page 1)*; ch 3, (sc in next sc, ch 3) around; join with slip st to first sc, finish off.

CUFF
Rnd 1: With **right** side facing and working in free loops of ch, join yarn with sc in marked ch of Sides; sc in next 10{11} chs; sc in each sc across last row of Instep; sc in each ch around; join with slip st to first sc: 30{32} sc.

Rnd 2 (Eyelet rnd)**:** Ch 4 **(counts as first dc plus ch 1)**, skip next sc, ★ dc in next sc, ch 1, skip next sc; repeat from ★ around; join with slip st to first dc: 15{16} ch-1 sps.

Rnd 3: Ch 1, sc in same st and in each ch-1 sp and each dc around; join with slip st to first sc, finish off: 30{32} sc.

Rnd 4: With **right** side facing and using smaller size hook, join Pink Fingering Weight Yarn with sc in first sc; ch 3, (sc in next sc, ch 3) around; join with slip st to first sc, finish off.

Make two Roses, page 11. Sew one Rose to Instep. Weave an 18" (45.5 cm) length of 1/4" (7 mm) wide ribbon through Eyelet rnd and tie ends into a bow.

HEADBAND
With Green Fingering Weight Yarn and smaller size hook, ch 8.

Row 1 (Right side)**:** Dc in fourth ch from hook **(3 skipped chs count as first dc)**, ch 2, skip next 2 chs, dc in last 2 chs: 4 dc and one ch-2 sp.

Note: Loop a short piece of yarn around any stitch to mark Row 1 as **right** side.

Row 2: Ch 3 **(counts as first dc)**, turn; dc in next dc, ch 2, dc in last 2 dc.

Repeat Row 2 until Headband measures head circumference minus 1" (2.5 cm), ending by working a **wrong** side row; finish off leaving a long end for sewing.

With **right** side together, sew free loops of beginning ch *(Fig. 1b, page 2)* to sts on last row.

Edging: With **right** side facing and using smaller size hook, join Pink Fingering Weight Yarn with sc in end of Row 1 *(see Joining With Sc, page 1)*; ch 3, sc in same row, (sc, ch 3, sc) in end of each row around; join with slip st to first sc, finish off.

Repeat on opposite side.

Make one Rose, page 11. Sew Rose over seam.

Beginning at seam, weave a 36" (91.5 cm) length of 1/4" (7 mm) wide ribbon through ch-2 sps. Tie ends into a bow behind Rose.

Continued on page 17.

AFGHAN
Finished Size: 33" x 35" (84 cm x 89 cm)

GAUGE SWATCH: 3¹/₂" (9 cm)
(straight edge to straight edge)
Work same as Motif.

Use Sport Weight Yarn and larger size hook throughout Afghan unless otherwise specified.

MOTIF (Make 94)
Rnd 1 (Right side)**:** With Pink, ch 2, 6 sc in second ch from hook; join with slip st to first sc.

Note: Loop a short piece of yarn around any stitch to mark Rnd 1 as **right** side.

Rnd 2: Work Beginning Popcorn in same st, ch 3, (work Popcorn in next sc, ch 3) around; join with slip st to top of Beginning Popcorn, finish off: 6 Popcorns and 6 ch-3 sps.

Rnd 3: With **right** side facing, join Green with slip st in any ch-3 sp; work (Beginning Cluster, ch 3, Cluster) in same sp, ch 1, ★ work (Cluster, ch 3, Cluster) in next ch-3 sp, ch 1; repeat from ★ around; join with slip st to top of Beginning Cluster: 12 Clusters and 12 sps.

Rnd 4: Slip st in first ch-3 sp, ch 3 **(counts as first dc, now and throughout)**, (2 dc, ch 2, 3 dc) in same sp, ch 1, 3 dc in next ch-1 sp, ch 1, ★ (3 dc, ch 2, 3 dc) in next ch-3 sp, ch 1, 3 dc in next ch-1 sp, ch 1; repeat from ★ around; join with slip st to first dc, finish off: 54 dc and 18 sps.

HALF MOTIF (Make 10)
Row 1: With Pink, ch 2, 5 sc in second ch from hook; do **not** join.

Row 2 (Right side)**:** Ch 4 **(counts as first dc plus ch 1, now and throughout)**, turn; work Popcorn in next sc, (ch 3, work Popcorn in next sc) twice, ch 1, dc in last sc; finish off: 4 sps.

Note: Mark Row 2 as **right** side.

Row 3: With **wrong** side facing, join Green with slip st in first dc; ch 4, work Cluster in next ch-1 sp, ch 1, [work (Cluster, ch 3, Cluster) in next ch-3 sp, ch 1] twice, work Cluster in next ch-1 sp, ch 1, dc in last dc: 6 Clusters, 2 dc, and 7 sps.

Row 4: Ch 4, turn; (3 dc in next ch-1 sp, ch 1) twice, (3 dc, ch 2, 3 dc) in next ch-3 sp, ch 1, 3 dc in next ch-1 sp, ch 1, (3 dc, ch 2, 3 dc) in next ch-3 sp, ch 1, (3 dc in next ch-1 sp, ch 1) twice, dc in last dc; finish off: 29 dc and 10 sps.

ASSEMBLY
With Green and using Placement Diagram as a guide, whipstitch Motifs and Half Motifs together **(Fig. 3, page 2)**, forming 6 horizontal strips of 9 Motifs each and 5 horizontal strips of 8 Motifs and 2 Half Motifs each; then whipstitch strips together in same manner.

PLACEMENT DIAGRAM

TRIM
First Side: With **right** side facing and working across long edge of Afghan, join Green with sc in first dc **after** corner ch-2 sp *(see Joining With Sc, page 1)*; sc in next 2 dc, (skip next ch-1 sp, sc in next 3 dc) twice, ★ skip next joining, working across end of rows on Half Motif, 2 sc in each of next 3 rows, sc in side of next 2 sc on Row 1, 2 sc in each of next 3 rows, skip next joining, sc in next 3 dc, (skip next ch-1 sp, sc in next 3 dc) twice; repeat from ★ 4 times **more**; finish off.

Second Side: Work same as First Side.

Edging: With **right** side facing and using smaller size hook, join Pink Fingering Weight Yarn with sc in first sc on either Side; ch 3, † (sc in next sc, ch 3) across; [skip next sp, (sc in next dc, ch 3) 3 times] 6 times, ★ skip next joining, (sc in next dc, ch 3) 3 times, [skip next sp, (sc in next dc, ch 3) 3 times] 5 times; repeat from ★ 7 times **more**, skip next ch-2 sp †; repeat from † to † once **more**; join with slip st to first sc, finish off.

3. SAY IT WITH FLOWERS

Shown on page 14.

MATERIALS

Item	Ounces	Yards	Grams	Meters
Coat				
White Fingering Weight Yarn	3¹/₂{4}	600{685}	100{110}	548.5{626.5}
Pink Fingering Weight Yarn	1/4	45	5	41
Green Fingering Weight Yarn		30		27.5
Dress				
White Fingering Weight Yarn	2¹/₂{3}	430{515}	70{90}	393{471}
Pink Fingering Weight Yarn		20		18.5
Green Fingering Weight Yarn		15		13.5
Bonnet				
White Fingering Weight Yarn	3/4{1}	130{170}	20{30}	119{155.5}
Pink Fingering Weight Yarn	1/3	60	10	55
Green Fingering Weight Yarn		15		13.5
Booties				
White Fingering Weight Yarn	1/3	60	10	55
Pink Fingering Weight Yarn		5		4.5
Green Fingering Weight Yarn		5		4.5
Afghan				
White Sport Weight Yarn	12¹/₂	1,140	360	1,042.5
Pink Sport Weight Yarn	2¹/₄	205	60	187.5
Green Sport Weight Yarn	1¹/₄	115	35	105

Crochet hooks, sizes D (3.25 mm) **and** G (4 mm) **or** sizes needed for gauge
Yarn needle
Sewing needle and thread
1/2" (12 mm) Buttons - 6
1/4" (7 mm) wide Ribbon - 3¹/₃ yards (3 meters)

Finished Size: 3 months and 6 months

Size Note: Instructions are written for size 3 months with size 6 months in braces { }. Instructions will be easier to read if you circle all the numbers pertaining to your size. If only one number is given, it applies to both sizes.

GAUGE: With Fingering Weight Yarn and smaller size hook, in pattern, (dc, ch 1, dc) 7 times and 10 rows = 3" (7.5 cm) 12 dc and 7 rows = 2" (5 cm)

Gauge Swatch: 3¹/₄"w x 3"h (8.5 cm x 7.5 cm) With Fingering Weight Yarn and smaller size hook, ch 27.
Row 1: (Dc, ch 1, dc) in sixth ch from hook, skip next 2 chs, ★ (dc, ch 1, dc) in next ch, skip next 2 chs; repeat from ★ 5 times **more**, dc in last ch: 7 ch-1 sps.

Rows 2-10: Ch 3, turn; (dc, ch 1, dc) in each ch-1 sp across, skip next dc, dc in next ch. Finish off.

STITCH GUIDE

> **TREBLE CROCHET** *(abbreviated tr)*
> YO twice, insert hook in dc indicated, YO and pull up a loop (4 loops on hook), (YO and draw through 2 loops on hook) 3 times.
>
> **BEGINNING SC DECREASE**
> Pull up a loop in first 2 sc, YO and draw through all 3 loops on hook **(counts as one sc)**.

Continued on page 19.

SC DECREASE
Pull up a loop in next 2 sc, YO and draw through all 3 loops on hook **(counts as one sc)**.

DC DECREASE (uses next 2 dc)
★ YO, insert hook in **next** dc, YO and pull up a loop, YO and draw through 2 loops on hook; repeat from ★ once **more**, YO and draw through all 3 loops on hook **(counts as one dc)**.

DOUBLE DC DECREASE (uses next 3 chs)
★ YO, insert hook in **next** ch, YO and pull up a loop, YO and draw through 2 loops on hook; repeat from ★ 2 times **more**, YO and draw through all 4 loops on hook **(counts as one dc)**.

BEGINNING CLUSTER (uses one sp)
Ch 2, ★ YO, insert hook in sp indicated, YO and pull up a loop, YO and draw through 2 loops on hook; repeat from ★ once **more**, YO and draw through all 3 loops on hook.

CLUSTER (uses one sp)
★ YO, insert hook in sp indicated, YO and pull up a loop, YO and draw through 2 loops on hook; repeat from ★ 2 times **more**, YO and draw through all 4 loops on hook.

PICOT
Ch 4, sc in fourth ch from hook.

COAT

Use Fingering Weight Yarn and smaller size hook throughout Coat.

BODICE
With White, ch 73{89}.

Row 1 (Right side): Dc in fourth ch from hook **(3 skipped chs count as first dc)** and in next 6{8} chs, (2 dc, ch 1, 2 dc) in next ch, ★ dc in next 17{21} chs, (2 dc, ch 1, 2 dc) in next ch; repeat from ★ 2 times **more**, dc in last 8{10} chs: 83{99} dc.

Note: Loop a short piece of yarn around any stitch to mark Row 1 as **right** side.

Rows 2-8: Ch 3 **(counts as first dc, now and throughout)**, turn; ★ dc in next dc and in each dc across to next ch-1 sp, (2 dc, ch 1, 2 dc) in ch-1 sp; repeat from ★ 3 times **more**, dc in next dc and in each dc across: 195{211} dc.

BODY
Size 3 Months Only - Row 1: Ch 3, turn; skip next dc, (dc, ch 1, dc) in next dc, † skip next dc, dc in next dc, (ch 1, dc in same st) twice, skip next dc, (dc, ch 1, dc) in next dc †; repeat from † to † across to within one dc of next ch-1 sp, skip next dc, (dc, ch 1, dc) in ch-1 sp, skip next 49 dc (armhole), (dc, ch 1, dc) in next ch-1 sp, skip next dc, (dc, ch 1, dc) in next dc, repeat from † to † across to within 3 dc of next ch-1 sp, skip next dc, dc in next dc, (ch 1, dc in same st) twice, skip next dc, (dc, ch 1, dc) in ch-1 sp, skip next 49 dc (armhole), (dc, ch 1, dc) in next ch-1 sp, skip next dc, (dc, ch 1, dc) in next dc, repeat from † to † across to last 2 dc, skip next dc, dc in last dc: 72 ch-1 sps.

Size 6 Months Only - Row 1: Ch 3, turn; ★ † skip next dc, (dc, ch 1, dc) in next dc, skip next dc, dc in next dc, (ch 1, dc in same st) twice †; repeat from † to † across to within one dc of next ch-1 sp, skip next dc, (dc, ch 1, dc) in ch-1 sp, skip next 53 dc (armhole), (dc, ch 1, dc) in next ch-1 sp; repeat from ★ once **more**, then repeat from † to † across to last 2 dc, skip next dc, dc in last dc: 79 ch-1 sps.

Both Sizes - Rows 2 thru 26{30}: Ch 3, turn; (dc, ch 1, dc) in next ch-1 sp and in each ch-1 sp across, dc in last dc.

Finish off.

SLEEVE
Rnd 1: With **right** side facing and working in end of Row 1 on Body, join White with slip st around first dc at armhole; ch 4 **(counts as first dc plus ch 1, now and throughout)**, dc around same st, (dc, ch 1, dc) around next dc; working in skipped dc on Bodice, (dc, ch 1, dc) in first dc, ★ skip next dc, (dc, ch 1, dc) in next dc; repeat from ★ around; join with slip st to first dc: 27{29} ch-1 sps.

Rnds 2 thru 16{18}: (Slip st, ch 4, dc) in next ch-1 sp, (dc, ch 1, dc) in next ch-1 sp and in each ch-1 sp around; join with slip st to first dc.

Rnd 17{19}: Slip st in next ch-1 sp, ch 1, sc in same sp and in each ch-1 sp around; join with slip st to first sc: 27{29} sc.

Rnd 18{20}: Ch 3, dc in next sc and in each sc around; join with slip st to first dc.

Rnd 19{21}: Ch 1, sc in same st and in each dc around; join with slip st to first sc, finish off.

Trim: With **right** side facing, join Pink with sc in any sc *(see Joining With Sc, page 1)*; ch 3, sc in same st, (sc, ch 3, sc) in next sc and in each sc around; join with slip st to first sc, finish off.

Repeat for second Sleeve.

NECK EDGE

With **right** side facing and working in free loops of beginning ch *(Fig. 1b, page 2)*, join White with slip st in first ch; ch 3, ★ dc in next ch and in each ch across to within one ch of corner ch, work double dc decrease; repeat from ★ 3 times **more**, dc in next 7{9} chs; do **not** finish off: 63{79} dc.

BUTTON BAND

Row 1: Ch 1; working in end of rows, work 64{70} sc evenly spaced across left front edge.

Rows 2 and 3: Ch 1, turn; sc in each sc across.

Finish off.

BUTTONHOLE BAND

Row 1: With **right** side facing and working in end of rows, join White with sc in last row of Body; work 63{69} sc evenly spaced across: 64{70} sc.

Row 2 (Buttonhole row)**:** Ch 1, turn; sc in first sc, ch 2, skip next sc (buttonhole), ★ sc in next 8 sc, ch 2, skip next sc (buttonhole); repeat from ★ once **more**, sc in each sc across.

Row 3: Ch 1, turn; sc in each sc and in each ch-2 sp across; finish off.

TRIM

With **right** side facing, join Pink with sc in first ch-1 sp on last row of Body; ch 3, sc in same sp, (sc, ch 3, sc) in next ch-1 sp and in each ch-1 sp across, sc in end of Row 1 on Buttonhole Band, ch 3, sc in first sc on Buttonhole Band, skip next sc, (sc, ch 3, sc) in next sc, [skip next 2 sc, (sc, ch 3, sc) in next sc] across to last sc, sc in last sc, ch 3; sc in first dc on Neck Edge, [skip next 2 dc, (sc, ch 3, sc) in next dc] across to last 2{3} dc, skip next 1{2} dc, sc in last dc, ch 3, sc in first sc on Button Band, (sc, ch 3, sc) in next sc, [skip next 2 sc, (sc, ch 3, sc) in next sc] across to last 2 sc, skip next sc, sc in last sc, ch 3, sc in end of Row 1 on Button Band; join with slip st to first sc, finish off.

APPLIQUÉS
FLOWER (Make 3)

Rnd 1: With Pink, ch 9, (dc, ch 5) 5 times in ninth ch from hook; join with slip st to fourth ch of beginning ch-9: 6 sts and 6 ch-5 sps.

Rnd 2: Ch 1, sc in same st, 5 dc in next ch-5 sp, (sc in next dc, 5 dc in next ch-5 sp) around; join with slip st to Back Loop Only of first sc *(Fig. 2, page 2)*: 36 sts.

Rnd 3: Ch 1, sc in same st, ch 5, skip next 5 dc, ★ sc in Back Loop Only of next sc, ch 5, skip next 5 dc; repeat from ★ around; join with slip st to **both** loops of first sc: 6 ch-5 sps.

Rnd 4: Ch 3, 7 dc in same st, sc in next ch-5 sp, (8 dc in next sc, sc in next ch-5 sp) around; join with slip st to first dc, finish off leaving a long end for sewing: 54 sts.

LEAF (Make 4)
With Green, ch 7.

Rnd 1 (Right side)**:** Sc in second ch from hook and in last 5 chs, ch 2; working in free loops of beginning ch, sc in first 6 chs, ch 2; join with slip st to first sc: 12 sc and 2 ch-2 sps.

Note: Mark Rnd 1 as **right** side.

Rnd 2: Ch 1, sc in same st and in each sc across to next ch-2 sp, (2 sc, ch 2, 2 sc) in ch-2 sp, sc in each sc across to next ch-2 sp, (2 sc, ch 2, 2 sc) in ch-2 sp; join with slip st to first sc: 20 sc and 2 ch-2 sps.

Rnds 3 and 4: Ch 1, sc in same st and in each sc across to next ch-2 sp, (2 sc, ch 2, 2 sc) in ch-2 sp, sc in each sc across to next ch-2 sp, (2 sc, ch 2, 2 sc) in ch-2 sp, sc in each sc across; join with slip st to first sc: 36 sc and 2 ch-2 sps.

Finish off, leaving a long end for sewing.

Using photo as a guide for placement, sew one Flower and one Leaf to each side of front. Sew one Flower and 2 Leaves to center back of Bodice (see inset, page 23).

Sew buttons to Button Band opposite buttonholes.

Continued on page 21.

DRESS

Use Fingering Weight Yarn and smaller size hook throughout Dress.

BODICE
With White, ch 60{75}.

Row 1 (Right side)**:** (Dc, ch 1, dc) in sixth ch from hook, **[**skip next 2 chs, (dc, ch 1, dc) in next ch**]** 0{1} time(s) *(see Zeros, page 1)*, skip next 2 chs, dc in next ch, (ch 1, dc in same st) 3 times, ★ **[**skip next 2 chs, (dc, ch 1, dc) in next ch**]** 4{5} times, skip next 2 chs, dc in next ch, (ch 1, dc in same st) 3 times; repeat from ★ 2 times **more**, **[**skip next 2 chs, (dc, ch 1, dc) in next ch**]** 1{2} time(s), skip next 2 chs, dc in last ch: 26{31} ch-1 sps.

Note: Loop a short piece of yarn around any stitch to mark Row 1 as **right** side.

Row 2: Ch 3 **(counts as first dc, now and throughout)**, turn; (dc, ch 1, dc) in next ch-1 sp and in each ch-1 sp across, skip last dc, dc in next ch.

Row 3: Ch 3, turn; (dc, ch 1, dc) in next 2{3} ch-1 sps, dc in next ch-1 sp, (ch 1, dc in same sp) 3 times, ★ (dc, ch 1, dc) in next 6{7} ch-1 sps, dc in next ch-1 sp, (ch 1, dc in same sp) 3 times; repeat from ★ 2 times **more**, (dc, ch 1, dc) in next 2{3} ch-1 sps, dc in last dc: 34{39} ch-1 sps.

Row 4: Ch 3, turn; (dc, ch 1, dc) in next ch-1 sp and in each ch-1 sp across, dc in last dc.

Row 5: Ch 3, turn; (dc, ch 1, dc) in next 3{4} ch-1 sps, dc in next ch-1 sp, (ch 1, dc in same sp) 3 times, ★ (dc, ch 1, dc) in next 8{9} ch-1 sps, dc in next ch-1 sp, (ch 1, dc in same sp) 3 times; repeat from ★ 2 times **more**, (dc, ch 1, dc) in next 3{4} ch-1 sps, dc in last dc: 42{47} ch-1 sps.

Row 6: Ch 3, turn; (dc, ch 1, dc) in next ch-1 sp and in each ch-1 sp across, dc in last dc.

Row 7: Ch 3, turn; (dc, ch 1, dc) in next 4{5} ch-1 sps, dc in next ch-1 sp, (ch 1, dc in same sp) 3 times, ★ (dc, ch 1, dc) in next 10{11} ch-1 sps, dc in next ch-1 sp, (ch 1, dc in same sp) 3 times; repeat from ★ 2 times **more**, (dc, ch 1, dc) in next 4{5} ch-1 sps, dc in last dc: 50{55} ch-1 sps.

Row 8: Ch 3, turn; (dc, ch 1, dc) in next ch-1 sp and in each ch-1 sp across, dc in last dc; do **not** finish off.

BODY
Rnd 1: Ch 3, turn; (dc, ch 1, dc) in next 6{7} ch-1 sps, ch 11 (armhole), skip next 12{13} ch-1 sps, (dc, ch 1, dc) in next 14{15} ch-1 sps, ch 11 (armhole), skip next 12{13} ch-1 sps, (dc, ch 1, dc) in next 6{7} ch-1 sps, dc in last dc, ch 2 (placket); join with slip st to first dc: 26{29} ch-1 sps and one ch-2.

Rnd 2: Ch 4 **(counts as first dc plus ch 1, now and throughout)**, do **not** turn; dc in same st, ★ (dc, ch 1, dc) in each ch-1 sp across to next ch-11, skip first 2 chs, **[**(dc, ch 1, dc) in next ch, skip next 2 chs**]** 3 times; repeat from ★ once **more**, (dc, ch 1, dc) in each ch-1 sp across, (dc, ch 1, dc) in last dc, skip last ch-2; join with slip st to first dc: 34{37} ch-1 sps.

Rnd 3: (Slip st, ch 4, dc) in next ch-1 sp, skip next dc, (dc, ch 1, dc) in sp **before** next dc, ★ (dc, ch 1, dc) in next ch-1 sp, skip next dc, (dc, ch 1, dc) in sp **before** next dc; repeat from ★ around; join with slip st to first dc: 68{74} ch-1 sps.

Rnds 4 thru 26{30}: (Slip st, ch 4, dc) in next ch-1 sp, (dc, ch 1, dc) in next ch-1 sp and in each ch-1 sp around; join with slip st to first dc.

Finish off.

Trim: With **right** side facing, join Pink with sc in any ch-1 sp *(see Joining With Sc, page 1)*; ch 3, sc in same sp, (sc, ch 3, sc) in next ch-1 sp and in each ch-1 sp around; join with slip st to first sc, finish off.

SLEEVE
Rnd 1: With **right** side facing and working in free loops *(Fig. 1b, page 2)* and sps across ch-11 at underarm, join White with sc in center ch; sc in next sp, sc in ch at base of next dc, sc in next sp, sc around dc on Rnd 1 of Body; working in skipped sts on Row 8 of Bodice, sc in first dc, (dc, ch 1, dc) in next 12{13} ch-1 sps, skip next dc, sc in next dc, sc around next dc on Rnd 1 of Body, sc in next sp and in ch at base of next dc, sc in last sp; join with slip st to first sc: 11 sc and 12{13} ch-1 sps.

Rnd 2: Ch 1, sc in same st and next 3 sc, sc decrease, (dc, ch 1, dc) in next ch-1 sp and in each ch-1 sp around to last 6 sts, skip next dc, sc decrease, sc in last 3 sc; join with slip st to first sc: 9 sc and 12{13} ch-1 sps.

Rnd 3: Ch 4, dc in same st, skip next 2 sc, (dc, ch 1, dc) in next sc and in each ch-1 sp around to last 5 sts, skip next 2 sts, (dc, ch 1, dc) in next sc, skip last 2 sc; join with slip st to first dc: 15{16} ch-1 sps.

Rnds 4 thru 7{8}: (Slip st, ch 4, dc) in next ch-1 sp, (dc, ch 1, dc) in next ch-1 sp and in each ch-1 sp around; join with slip st to first dc.

Finish off.

Trim: With **right** side facing, join Pink with sc in any ch-1 sp; ch 3, sc in same sp, (sc, ch 3, sc) in next ch-1 sp and in each ch-1 sp around; join with slip st to first sc, finish off.

Repeat for second Sleeve.

RIGHT PLACKET
Row 1: With **right** side facing and working in end of rows along right back edge, join White with sc in Row 1 of Bodice; work 17 sc evenly spaced across: 18 sc.

Rows 2 and 3: Ch 1, turn; sc in each sc across.

Finish off.

LEFT PLACKET
Row 1: With **right** side facing and working in end of rows across left back edge, join White with sc in Rnd 1 of Body; work 17 sc evenly spaced across: 18 sc.

Row 2 (Buttonhole row)**:** Ch 1, turn; sc in first sc, ch 2, skip next sc (buttonhole), ★ sc in next 5 sc, ch 2, skip next sc (buttonhole); repeat from ★ once **more**, sc in last 4 sc.

Row 3: Ch 1, turn; sc in each sc and in each ch-2 sp across; finish off.

Lapping Left Placket over Right Placket, sew bottom of Plackets to ch-2 on Rnd 1 of Body.

NECK EDGING
With **right** side facing, join Pink with sc in end of Row 3 of Left Placket; ch 3, skip next row, sc in next row; working in sps across beginning ch, (sc, ch 3, sc) in each sp across; sc in end of Row 1 on Right Placket, ch 3, skip next row, sc in last row; finish off.

Sew buttons to Right Placket opposite buttonholes.

APPLIQUÉS
FLOWER
Work same as Flower, page 20.

LEAF (Make 2)
Work same as Leaf, page 20.

FINISHING
Working across front of Dress, weave one 36" (91.5 cm) length of ribbon through sts on Rnd 1 of Body, beginning at one underarm and ending at opposite underarm. Weave another 36" (91.5 cm) length of ribbon in same manner across back of Dress. Tie ribbons into a bow at each side.

Using photo as a guide for placement:
  Sew Flower and Leaves to front of Dress.
  With Green, work chain stitch stem *(Figs. 4a & b, page 2)*.
  Tie a 12" (30.5 cm) length of ribbon into a bow around stem.

BONNET
Use Fingering Weight Yarn and smaller size hook throughout Bonnet.

With White, ch 45{51}.

Row 1: (Dc, ch 1, dc) in sixth ch from hook, ★ skip next 2 chs, (dc, ch 1, dc) in next ch; repeat from ★ across to last 3 chs, skip next 2 chs, dc in last ch: 13{15} ch-1 sps.

Row 2 (Right side)**:** Ch 3 **(counts as first dc, now and throughout)**, turn; (dc, ch 1, dc) in next ch-1 sp, ★ skip next dc, (dc, ch 1, dc) in sp **before** next dc and in next ch-1 sp; repeat from ★ across, skip last dc, dc in next ch: 25{29} ch-1 sps.

Note: Loop a short piece of yarn around any stitch to mark Row 2 as **right** side.

Rows 3 thru 14{16}: Ch 3, turn; (dc, ch 1, dc) in next ch-1 sp and in each ch-1 sp across, dc in last dc.

Finish off.

Ties and Trim: With Pink, ch 55{60} (tie), slip st in second ch from hook and in each ch across; with **right** side of Bonnet facing, (sc, ch 3, sc) in first dc and in each ch-1 sp across to last 2 dc, skip next dc, (sc, ch 3, sc) in last dc, ch 55{60} (tie), turn; slip st in second ch from hook and in each ch across, slip st in next sc; finish off.

Continued on page 23.

APPLIQUÉS
FLOWER (Make 2)
Work same as Flower, page 20.

LEAF (Make 2)
Work same as Leaf, page 20.

BOW
With Pink, ch 13.

Row 1 (Right side): Sc in second ch from hook and in each ch across: 12 sc.

Note: Mark Row 1 as **right** side.

Rows 2-60: Ch 1, turn; sc in each sc across.

Finish off, leaving a long end for sewing.

With **right** side together, sew free loops of beginning ch *(Fig. 1b, page 2)* to sc on last row.

KNOT
With Pink, ch 9.

Row 1 (Right side): Sc in second ch from hook and in each ch across: 8 sc.

Note: Mark Row 1 as **right** side.

Rows 2-16: Ch 1, turn; sc in each sc across.

Finish off, leaving a long end for sewing.

With **right** side together, sew free loops of beginning ch to sc on last row.

FINISHING
Slip Bow inside of Knot with Bow seam at center and Knot seam at back; tack together at back.

Using photo as a guide:
  Sew end of rows at back of Knot to ends of Rows 1-4 on Bonnet.
  Tack folded edges of Bow to Row 5 on Bonnet.
  Sew one Flower and one Leaf to each side of Bonnet (see Inset below).

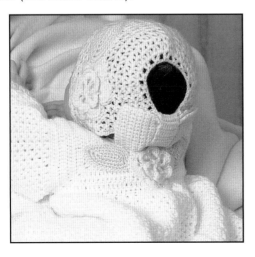

BOOTIES
Use Fingering Weight Yarn and smaller size hook throughout Booties.

TOE
Rnd 1 (Right side): With White, ch 4, 8{9} dc in fourth ch from hook; join with slip st to top of beginning ch-4: 9{10} sts.

Note: Loop a short piece of yarn around any stitch to mark Rnd 1 as **right** side.

Rnd 2: Ch 3 **(counts as first dc, now and throughout)**, dc in same st, 2 dc in next dc and in each dc around; join with slip st to first dc: 18{20} dc.

Rnd 3: Ch 3, dc in same st and in next dc, (2 dc in next dc, dc in next dc) around; join with slip st to first dc: 27{30} dc.

Rnds 4 thru 5{6}: Ch 3, dc in next dc and in each dc around; join with slip st to first dc; do **not** finish off.

SIDES
Row 1: Ch 3, dc in next 21{23} dc, leave remaining 5{6} dc unworked: 22{24} dc.

Row 2: Ch 3, turn; dc in next dc and in each dc across.

Row 3: Ch 4 **(counts as first tr)**, turn; dc in next dc and in each dc across to last dc, tr in last dc.

Rows 4-6: Ch 3, turn; dc in next dc and in each st across.

Row 7: Ch 3, turn; dc in next 6{7} dc, work dc decrease 4 times, dc in last 7{8} dc: 18{20} dc.

Row 8: Ch 3, turn; dc in next dc and in each dc across.

Joining Row: Ch 1, turn; folding Row 8 in half so that **wrong** sides are together, matching sts and working through **both** thicknesses, slip st in each st across; finish off.

TRIM
With **right** side facing, join Green with sc in seam *(see Joining With Sc, page 1)*; work 2 sc in end of first 5 rows, (slip st, ch 1, 5 sc, slip st) around tr on next row, 2 sc in end of next 2 rows; working in unworked sc on Rnd 5{6} of Toe, sc in next 5{6} sc, work 2 sc in end of next 2 rows, (slip st, ch 1, 5 sc, slip st) around tr on next row, work 2 sc in end of next 5 rows; join with slip st to first sc, finish off.

FLOWER

With Pink, ch 3; join with slip st to form a ring.

Rnd 1 (Right side)**:** (Ch 3, dc, ch 3, slip st) 6 times in ring; finish off leaving a long end for sewing.

Using photo as a guide for placement, sew Flower to Toe.

Weave an 18" (45.5 cm) length of ribbon through rows on Sides, beginning and ending with Row 3.

AFGHAN

Finished Size: 37" (94 cm) square

Use Sport Weight Yarn and larger size hook throughout Afghan.

GAUGE: In pattern,
(dc, ch 1, dc) 5 times = 3" (7.5 cm);
8 rows = $3^{1}/_{2}$" (9 cm)

Gauge Swatch: $3^{1}/_{2}$" (9 cm) square
Ch 21.
Work same as Afghan Center for 8 rows.
Finish off.

CENTER

With White, ch 141.

Row 1 (Right side)**:** (Dc, ch 1, dc) in sixth ch from hook, ★ skip next 2 chs, (dc, ch 1, dc) in next ch; repeat from ★ across to last 3 chs, skip next 2 chs, dc in last ch: 45 ch-1 sps.

Note: Loop a short piece of yarn around any stitch to mark Row 1 as **right** side.

Row 2: Ch 3 **(counts as first dc, now and throughout)**, turn; (dc, ch 1, dc) in next ch-1 sp and in each ch-1 sp across, skip last dc, dc in next ch.

Rows 3-63: Ch 3, turn; (dc, ch 1, dc) in next ch-1 sp and in each ch-1 sp across, dc in last dc.

Finish off.

BORDER
TRIANGLE (Make 24)

With Pink, ch 5; join with slip st to form a ring.

Rnd 1 (Right side)**:** Work (Beginning Cluster, ch 3, Cluster) in ring, ch 5, ★ work (Cluster, ch 3, Cluster) in ring, ch 5; repeat from ★ once **more**; join with slip st to top of Beginning Cluster, finish off: 6 sps.

Note: Mark Rnd 1 as **right** side.

Rnd 2: With **right** side facing, join Green with slip st in any ch-5 sp; work (Beginning Cluster, ch 5, Cluster) in same sp, ch 3, sc in next ch-3 sp, ch 3, ★ work (Cluster, ch 5, Cluster) in next ch-5 sp, ch 3, sc in next ch-3 sp, ch 3; repeat from ★ once **more**; join with slip st to top of Beginning Cluster, finish off: 9 sps.

Rnd 3: With **right** side facing, join White with slip st in any ch-5 sp; ch 3, (3 dc, ch 3, 4 dc) in same sp, dc in next Cluster, (3 dc in next ch-3 sp, dc in next st) twice, ★ (4 dc, ch 3, 4 dc) in next ch-5 sp, dc in next Cluster, (3 dc in next ch-3 sp, dc in next st) twice; repeat from ★ once **more**; join with slip st to first dc, finish off: 51 dc (17 dc **each** side) and 3 ch-3 sps.

JOINING

With **right** side facing, join White with sc in any ch-3 sp on first Triangle *(see Joining With Sc, page 1)*; sc in same sp and in each dc across to next ch-3 sp, 2 sc in ch-3 sp; ★ with **right** side of **next** Triangle facing, 2 sc in any ch-3 sp, sc in each dc across to next ch-3 sp, 2 sc in ch-3 sp; repeat from ★ 22 times **more**, finish off.

With **right** sides together, pin first six Triangles along one edge of Center, beginning with first 2 sc on Joining at corner and last 2 sc on sixth Triangle at next corner. Continue in same manner around Center, having six Triangles on each side.
With White, sew Triangles to Center.

Continued on page 25.

EDGING

Rnd 1: With **right** side facing, join White with sc in unworked ch-3 sp at point of any Triangle; work Picot, sc in same sp, ★ † sc in next 17 dc and in next ch-3 sp, work Picot, sc in next ch-3 sp on next Triangle and in next 17 dc †, (sc, work Picot, sc) in next ch-3 sp; repeat from ★ 22 times **more**, then repeat from † to † once; join with slip st to first sc.

Rnd 2: (Slip st, ch 1, sc) in ch-4 sp of next Picot, ★ † ch 3, (skip next sc, sc in next sc, ch 3) 7 times, skip next 5 sc, sc in ch-4 sp of next Picot, ch 3, skip next 5 sc, (sc in next sc, ch 3, skip next sc) 7 times †, sc in ch-4 sp of next Picot; repeat from ★ 22 times **more**, then repeat from † to † once; join with slip st to first sc, finish off.

APPLIQUÉS
FLOWER (Make 3)

Rnds 1-4: Work same as Flower, page 20; do **not** finish off: 54 sts.

Rnd 5: Ch 1, sc in same st, ★ † dc in next dc, tr in next dc, 3 tr in each of next 2 dc, tr in next dc, dc in next dc, sc in next dc, slip st in next sc †, sc in next dc; repeat from ★ 4 times **more**, then repeat from † to † once; join with slip st to first sc, finish off leaving a long end for sewing.

LEAF (Make 4)
Work same as Leaf, page 20.

BOW
First Side
With Pink, ch 13.

Row 1: Sc in second ch from hook and in each ch across: 12 sc.

Row 2 (Right side)**:** Ch 1, turn; sc in each sc across.

Note: Mark Row 2 as **right** side.

Rows 3-16: Ch 1, turn; sc in each sc across.

Finish off, leaving a long end for sewing.

Second Side
Row 1: With **wrong** side facing and working in free loops of beginning ch *(Fig. 1b, page 2)*, join Pink with sc in first ch; sc in next ch and in each ch across: 12 sc.

Rows 2-16: Ch 1, turn; sc in each sc across.

Finish off, leaving a long end for sewing.

With **right** side together, sew last row of Sides together.

Knot
With Pink and leaving a long end for sewing, ch 9.

Row 1: Sc in second ch from hook and in each ch across: 8 sc.

Row 2 (Right side)**:** Ch 1, turn; sc in each sc across.

Note: Mark Row 2 as **right** side.

Rows 3-16: Ch 1, turn; sc in each sc across.

Finish off, leaving a long end for sewing.

With **right** side together, sew free loops of beginning ch to sc on last row.

Streamer (Make 2)
With Pink, ch 5.

Row 1: Sc in second ch from hook and in each ch across: 4 sc.

Rows 2 and 3: Ch 1, turn; 2 sc in first sc, sc in each sc across to last sc, 2 sc in last sc: 8 sc.

Rows 4-14: Ch 1, turn; sc in each sc across.

Row 15: Ch 1, turn; work beginning sc decrease, sc in last 6 sc: 7 sc.

Row 16: Ch 1, turn; sc in each sc across to last 2 sc, sc decrease: 6 sc.

Rows 17-20: Repeat Rows 15 and 16 twice: 2 sc.

Row 21: Ch 1, turn; work beginning sc decrease; finish off: one sc.

FINISHING
Slip Bow inside of Knot with Bow seam at center and Knot seam at back; tack together at back. Sew Row 1 of each Streamer to wrong side of Knot.

Using photo, page 26, as a guide for placement:
  Sew Bow, Flowers, and Leaves to Center.
  With Green, work chain stitch stems *(Figs. 4a & b, page 2)*.